Writing

The Arts and Living

Leonee Ormond

General editors for the series John Fleming and Hugh Honour

London: Her Majesty's Stationery Office

Acknowledgements

In preparing a booklet which covers such a wide range of subjects and periods, I have become indebted to a large number of people, all of whom have given most generously of their time and expertise.

I owe particular thanks to Professor Julian Brown, of King's College, London, who has helped me through the minefield of the early history of writing. He is, however, in no way to be held responsible for any errors and omissions in dealing with such a complex subject.

Within the Victoria and Albert Museum, I should particularly like to thank Mr. John Mallet, Mr. Michael Archer, Mr. Timothy Clifford (now City Art Gallery, Manchester) and Miss Charlotte Sillivan of the Department of Ceramics, Mr. Clive Wainright and Miss Gillian Walkling of the Department of Furniture and Woodwork, and Mr. Anthony Burton of the Library.

Among the many others outside the Museum whom I wish to thank are Miss Janet Cowen, Mr. and Mrs. Hylton Bayntun-Coward, Professor Angus Easson, Dr. David Nokes, Mr. and Mrs. A. V. B. Norman, Mr. Richard Proudfoot, Professor J. P. W. Rogers and Mrs. Elaine Calnan.

Finally, I must thank my husband for his help and encouragement, and my Aunt, Miss M. A. Woods, without whose kindness this booklet would never have been completed.

Leonée Ormond

With the following exceptions all the objects illustrated are from the Victoria and Albert Museum. Fig.1 British Museum; Fig.6 Staatliche Museen, Berlin; Fig.16 Louvre, Paris; Fig. 32 Science Museum.

Design by HMSO Graphic Design

ISBN 0 11 290282 0

Contents

Figure 1. Clay tablet written in pictographic script showing a list of personal names, with each is a number expressed by semi-circles. The reverse shows what is recorded i.e. oxen and cows. From Uruk Sumer. c.1300 B.C.

1 Beginnings

It is perhaps because writing is such a universal occupation that we take its implements for granted. We recognise the importance of easel, brushes and canvas for the artist far more readily than we do the pen, the inkwell or the desk for the author. Yet the impact of these materials on the history of civilisation has been incalculable. Imagine what might have happened if ink had never been discovered, and writing had been restricted to incised symbols on stone or clay. What would Homer have done with a typewriter? How would modern business cope if only the quill pen existed?

At every stage in the history of civilisation the possibilities of the written word have been dependent on the materials available. The step from reed pen and papyrus to quill pen and paper may not seem a very large one, but the increased facility of the one encouraged the spread of writing on an unprecedented scale. Size of paper, flexibility of nib, quality of ink, all these things have had an effect on what an individual writer could do and say. The change brought about by the ball-point pen in our day has been so complete that it is difficuit to recapture the time of messy inkwells, blots and broken nibs. The impact of the typewriter on grammatical construction has been scarcely less dramatic, and many authors are quite incapable of writing without its aid.

It is not, of course, just a question of what we write with, but what we write at. Objects, like inkwells and desks, provide the indispensable environment of the writer. Most of us have just as strong prejudices about the pens we write with as about the desks at which we sit. Comfort, ease and efficiency are the adjuncts to fluency of thought and hand. The desk is quite a recent and a largely Western development. Writers of the past have often had to put up with very basic supports, and very primitive containers. The medieval monk was expected to produce calligraphy of the finest quality in the most austere conditions. Could Dickens have written *Pickwick Papers* with a board on his knee? And what would St. Jerome have made of Dickens' cosy and well-appointed study?

Many of the materials associated with writing have attracted the attention of designers and craftsmen. They have become objects of beauty in their own right, reflecting the style of the time at which they were produced. It is not the aim of the present booklet to disparage their artistic importance. Rather it is to set them in the context of social and intellectual history, to show that, however exquisite and beautifully made they may have been, they were actually used, and that changes in design were often prompted by changes in function as well as by changes of style. The Louis Quinze desk is now a show-piece, but somebody once sat at it, thought at it, wrote at it. Why was it like that? What factors determined its shape and function? These are some of the questions this booklet will seek to answer.

In prehistoric times, man's instinctive desire to communicate was satisfied by scratching signs in the sand, or by drawing symbols and animals in more permanent form on the walls of caves. The meaning of these drawings is obscure, but anyone who has gone underground will recognise their haunting and mysterious properties. Later, these signs became formalised into patterns, which could be recognised and interpreted by others. Probably the earliest experiments in writing as such are the clay tablets made by the Sumerians *[fig.1]*, a race living in the South of Mesopotamia, which is often regarded as the cradle of civilisation. Some of these tablets can be dated to as early as 3100 B.C. They show small pictorial shapes, first cut with a triangular reed pen, and then baked into the mud.

While Sumerian writing, known as cuneiform from the Latin word cuneus, a wedge, spread from the Sumerians to other countries in the Near East, the ancient Egyptians were developing their own pictorial system of writing, the hieroglyphic. Hieroglyphics were small pictures of men, animals and objects which were painted or carved onto monuments. The unwieldy hieroglyphic style remained a largely formal and sacred one, and two more rapid systems of writing were later developed by the Egyptians, the heiratic and the demotic. These were 'written' with a brush pen made from a rush onto papyrus, an early form of paper made from the reeds growing near the Nile Delta. The stems of the reeds were cut into longitudinal strips which were then pressed together to form a flat surface. After being polished to provide a writing surface, the papyrus was made into rolls of anything from thirty to one hundred feet long. Papyrus was normally rolled up, and stored in containers of wood or bark.

The Egyptians were not the only ancient people to develop the idea of writing with a brush. A similar development from pictorial to symbolic forms can also be traced in China, and the writing brush made from stiff hair was evolved there around the third century B.C. Chinese writing became a highly developed calligraphic art, and examples of it were hung up as decoration in the same spirit as pictures. The calligraphic tradition remains strong in Japan, whose culture owes much to China. A typical Japanese writing box will contain an assortment of delicate brushes and a solid block of ink usually incised with a decorative design; this is rubbed onto a stone and carefully mixed with water at the same time to produce a fine ink [fig.2]. The Japanese are also notable for the quality of their papers.

Figure 2.
Japanese writing box. Porcelain and gold lacquer on natural wood. Attributed to Hanzon. Late seventeenth century.
The figure is of the poet Hitomaro (c.680–c.710 A.D.), and was added in the early eighteenth century. Inside the box are a copper water bottle and an ink stone.

The Egyptians made use of a rush pen with its ends frayed like a brush. Greek and Roman writers, on the other hand, sharpened a reed to a point, achieving a much tauter form of writing as a result. The reed pen had to be constantly resharpened, like a pencil, and it was often reduced to a quarter of its length before being abandoned. The reed pen had largely disappeared from the Latin world by about 800 A.D., but it was revived in fifteenth century Italy when scholars began to study Greek. Portraits of Erasmus, the great Renaissance scholar, often show him writing with such a pen, one end finely pointed, the other cut short and squared off *[fig.3]*. In the late eighteenth century, William Blake could refer to himself, albeit allegorically, as writing with a 'rural pen' made from a 'hollow reed'.

The most common alternative to the reed pen was the stylus or metal pen, employed in classical times for writing letters onto a tablet. These tablets were originally made of wood, with the writing side hollowed out and coated with wax, so that the letters could be erased and the tablet re-used. The stylus, pointed at one end, was often flattened at the other as an erasing instrument. The tablet and stylus were also ideal for educational purposes, and they performed the same service for the Roman schoolboy as the more recent slate and slate pencil. Unwieldy as they were, tablets were sometimes joined together in order to provide more space for writing. In a famous Pompeian fresco of a young girl, said to be a poetess, she is holding a stylus in one hand with a group of tablets or codex in the other, like a primitive book.

From late Roman and Byzantine times, tablets were often made of ivory as well as of wood, and the outsides were delicately carved and decorated. The use of such tablets can be traced well into the medieval period, and in remote districts it lasted much longer. The example illustrated here was made in Germany in the fourteenth century, and shows two lovers out hawking *[fig.4]*. Some modern scholars think it probable that Geoffrey Chaucer, the fourteenth century poet, composed his poetry on wax tablets, later transferring his text to the more durable medium of vellum or parchment.

Figure 3. Albrecht Dürer. *Portrait of Erasmus.* 1526.

Animal skin was already being used as an alternative to papyrus in Egypt by about 2700 B.C. Skin was far more durable than papyrus, and, over the years, methods of treating it became more sophisticated. Parchment, made from the skin of a lamb, was in common use in Rome by the first century A.D., and the finest of medieval manuscripts were often written on vellum, made from the skin of a calf. The soft surface made writing and illumination easier, and allowed for erasure and alteration.

If the development of parchment represented one revolution in writing, another was the introduction of the quill or feather pen, which seems to have occurred in the post-Roman period. The quill pen was usually made from the wing feather of a goose, although other birds like swans, crows and turkeys were occasionally used. The end of the feather was cut and shaped to a point, which was then split to allow the free flow of ink. As it became blunt, the feather could be recut, as long as the broader part of the stem remained intact. Some writers recommended heating the end of the quill in hot ashes in order to harden the point. In comparison with the reed pen, the quill was infinitely more flexible, and its unique quality ensured it a position of primacy until the nineteenth century. The very word 'pen', comes from the Latin penna, meaning a feather. Attempts to produce a flexible metal pen as a replacement for the quill resulted in disappointments for many optimistic inventors.

Figure 4.
Ivory cover from a set of writing tablets, showing lovers hawking. Germany, upper Rhine. Mid fourteenth century.

2 The Middle Ages

The greatest exponents of the art of writing with the quill pen were unquestionably the medieval scribes. Laboriously copying manuscripts of the Bible and the works of the Church Fathers throughout the monastic houses of Europe they encouraged the habit of writing, and with it the spread of learning and knowledge. The Renaissance would be unthinkable without their patient and often repetitive efforts over the course of many centuries. We know very little about the monastic scribes before the ninth century, but it is possible to build up a picture of their life in the early middle ages. At first, they carried on their work of copying on the north side of the cloisters, where the church wall gave them some protection against the weather. At a later date, when the cloisters themselves were sometimes glazed, separate desks or carrels were provided. Some monastic houses boasted a scriptorium, a special room set aside for the purpose of writing. There the armarius, the monk responsible for the writing materials, issued equipment to the scribes, desks, ink, parchment, pens, knives, pumice-stone and rulers. The first step was to smooth out the page of vellum with pumice-stone. Next the lines were ruled. Finally, the scribe would begin writing, weighting down the pages of the book from which he was copying. No artificial light was allowed in the scriptorium in case of fire, nor were the monks permitted to talk. Thus, the scribe would sit for as much as six hours in silence, carefully copying the work in front of him. The rules of the scriptoria extended to the style of writing as well as the technique. An expert can often tell both the date and provenance of a manuscript from the hand in which it is written.

Representations of medieval scribes usually show them with pens in the right hand, knives in the left. The latter were used not only for sharpening pens, but also for erasing mistakes and for steadying the sheet as it was written. The ink, made from oak galls and iron, was apparently never blotted, but allowed to dry naturally to a deep black colour. Iron gall ink was still in use in Shakespeare's day. In a play on the word, Sir Toby Belch advises Sir Andrew Aguecheek to issue his challenge in the following terms: 'Let there be gall enough in thy ink, though thou write with a goose-pen' (*Twelfth Night.*)

Looking at a medieval manuscript, with its intricacy and beauty of line, it is easy to forget the grinding, monotonous daily labour and effort involved in its production. Medieval scribes were a querulous lot, and they were under no illusions about the drudgery of their work. One eighth century scribe reported that

ignorant people think the scribe's profession an easy one. Three fingers are engaged in writing, the two eyes in looking; your tongue pronounces the words and the whole body toils.

Another asks for the reader's prayers, and tells him,

Be careful with your fingers; don't put them on my writing. You do not know what it is to write. It is excessive drudgery: it crooks your back, dims your sight, twists your stomach and sides.

In the early middle ages, the activity of writing was so universally associated with the clergy that the word, clerk (one who writes), evolved directly from the term, cleric. As time passed, however, the monasteries had to depend to an increasing extent on professional scribes or scriveners, who were also employed by merchants, men of property and by the court. In a poem fiercely addressed to his scrivener, Adam, Chaucer urged him to be more careful and conscientious:

> Adam scriveyn, if ever it thee bifalle
> Boece or Troilus to wryten newe,
> Under thy lokkes thou most have the scalle,
> But after my making thou wryte trewe.
> So ofte a daye I mot thy werk renewe,
> Hit to correcte and eek to rubbe and scrape;
> And al is through thy negligence and rape.

A later poet, Thomas Hoccleve, had worked as a scrivener in the office of the Privy Seal in the early fifteenth century. He showed as little enthusiasm for the task as those monks quoted above, claiming that twenty-three years of writing had impaired his eyesight, and left his body infirm: 'Only those who have not written every day would call the clerk's life a game', he says, regretting that he was not even permitted to sing at his work like a craftsman.

Some medieval clerks travelled from place to place, carrying pen and ink with them. William Caxton, the first English printer, writes in the fifteenth century of a scrivener with his 'penner and an ynk-horn on his gurdel', the penner being a case for quill pens and knife, and the inkhorn his portable inkpot, made of animal horn. The word passed into common usage, and Laurence Sterne, the eighteenth century novelist, speaks colloquially of 'unscrewing his inkhorn' in *Tristram Shandy*.

It is not surprising that few writing materials survive in Western Europe from the Middle Ages. An ivory pen case dating from the eleventh century can be seen in the British Museum, but the quill pen itself was eminently expendable, and penknives and inkwells were not regarded as objects of value. We can, however, form a vivid impression of medieval scribes and their equipment from contemporary illuminations. Sometimes depicted simply as clerks, more commonly cast in the role of evangelists or church fathers, they sit at their steeply angled desks surrounded by the tools of their trade. In one of the fifteenth century examples illustrated here, St. John sits in his carrel composing his gospel on a single sheet of paper, while a symbolic eagle stands beside him *[pl.1]*. In the second, the saint is shown in open country, against a background of castles, river and trees. He is writing in an already bound book, which was not common practice, while the eagle holds a portable inkpot and pen-holder *[pl.2]*.

3 The Renaissance

The tradition of portraying scribes in this way continued into the Renaissance period. St. Jerome was a popular subject for contemporary treatment of this kind. In Dürer's engraving of 1514, Jerome is transformed into a German scholar of the Reformation, seated at a small sloping portable desk, with a round inkpot and a quill pen, and with books scattered everywhere about the room. Candles, an hour-glass, letters received, and supplies of ink housed in bottles can be seen on the high shelves behind him *[fig.5]*. Significantly, Dürer's print was later adapted as a portrait of Martin Luther, with only the features altered.

As the idea of portraiture developed during the Renaissance, it became customary to depict sitters in terms of their status and profession. Kings were painted with the symbols of authority, soldiers with the attributes of war, and so on. Writers and philosophers were commonly shown pen in hand, often in attitudes of thought or inspiration. Pen and inkpot also appeared in the portraits of statesmen and lawyers as evidence of a ceaseless public activity. The most interesting representation of writing materials, however, occurs in pictures of businessmen and money-lenders. There are no portraits of this type as memorable as those of the German Hansa merchants in London, painted by Hans Holbein in the early 1530s. German realism and Renaissance monumentality combine to produce a keen sense of individual character seen in terms of a specific mercantile and middle-class background. The greatest of these portraits shows the Danzig merchant, George Gisze, standing behind a table covered with a turkey-rug. Among the objects on it can be seen pens, inkwells, seal, signet ring, a box with money, scissors and a pounce pot. This last item contained resin which was shaken over the page of writing paper to prevent the ink

Figure 5. Albrecht Dürer. *St. Jerome*. 1514.

from soaking through. Behind are bills, letters, paper wafers used for sealing letters, books, boxes, scales, and string. None of this detail, however, detracts from the sensitive and moving characterisation of Gisze himself *[fig.6]*.

The letter which Gisze is opening is made of paper, which had by this date replaced parchment or vellum for ordinary use. The discovery of paper is usually attributed to the Chinese, who were manufacturing it from rags and vegetable matter by the second century B.C. The Arabs were conversant with the

Figure 6. Hans Holbein. *The Hanseatic Merchant George Gisze of Danzig.* 1532.

technique of producing it by the eighth century A.D., and it was first introduced into Europe through the Moorish settlements of Sicily and Southern Spain. Paper is only one instance of the important part played by the Islamic world in the development of writing materials. Early painted representations of their universities confirm the impression of elegance and sophistication given by surviving inkwells and pen boxes. Engraved and inlaid bronze inkwells, dating from the twelfth and thirteenth centuries, contrast sharply with those of horn and leather in medieval Europe. Islamic inkwells are frequently inscribed with texts, either telling us about the owner, or, as in one early sixteenth century Persian example, expressing a wish that 'the scribe may write a royal cypher for this inkwell in Indian ink and perpetually give the water of life' *[fig.7]*. A fourteenth century Egyptian brass writing case, decorated with gold and silver, is again delicately patterned, with finely wrought hinges *[fig.7]*.

Paper, so long known in the Islamic world, was increasingly used in Europe from the twelfth century onwards. Made from rags, it had begun to replace parchment by the fourteenth century. In England it was employed at first for less important documents, but eventually it superseded parchment entirely. Until the seventeenth century it was almost all imported, chiefly from Normandy and the Low Countries. The popularity of paper can be directly related to the rise in literacy and the consequent demand for cheap forms of writing material. As society became more organised and complex the need for documents, letters and books became even more pressing. The written word invaded all spheres of life, and writing became no longer a special skill but something expected of every educated man. Facility in writing was another thing. The famous Paston letters, written between members of a wealthy Norfolk family

Figure 7 (left). Brass inkwell with silver inlay, signed Mirak Hosayn Yazdi, probably West Iran, early sixteenth century; *(right)* brass writing case, damascened with gold and silver; Egyptian, fourteenth century; Inscribed with Mamluk titles.

Plate 1. St. John writing his gospel. French book of Hours. c.1400.

Plate 2. St. John writing his gospel. Book of Hours of Marguerite
de Foix, c.1475.

Plate 4. Ebony inkstand overlaid with silver. Engraved by Theodor de Bry of Frankfurt. Late sixteenth century.

Plate 3 (opposite).
Wooden writing box, decorated with the arms of Henry VIII and Catherine of Aragon. About 1529.

at the end of the fifteenth century, provide evidence of the difficulty experienced by correspondents. They usually drafted the letters in rough before proceeding to a fair copy. Whenever possible, they much preferred to use the services of an amanuensis.

As the habit of writing spread through the upper and middle classes, a new item of furniture makes its appearance in the domestic interior. This is the writing box, a small transportable object, which could be placed on a table when in use. John Paston speaks of a 'wryghting box of cypresse' in one of his letters, but we can only guess at the appearance of these late medieval examples. One of the earliest to survive is the superb Renaissance writing box of the early sixteenth century, bearing the arms of Henry VIII and Catherine of Aragon for whom it was presumably designed. Decorated outside with figures from classical mythology, it has compartments inside for pens and inkwells, as well as three small drawers. The sloping top of the box was designed as a small writing top. The box combines great beauty of form with a strong functional sense *[pl.3]*.

The present leather covering of Henry VIII's writing box was added to it at a later date; it was probably originally covered with either painted leather or with velvet. The inventories of Henry's palaces refer to a number of table desks like the two 'of waynscott (oak) standing in the myddes of ij (two) tables couered wt vellouet ... (velvet) wherein is iij (three) litle boxes of Silver for Inke'. Henry VIII's daughter, Elizabeth I, is recorded as owning two little writing cabinets of 'exquisite work' as well as a 'desk of timber couered wth crimsen veluet garnished wth lace and fringe of siluer and nayles siluered wth yronworke', which was made for her in 1565 by her coffer-maker, John Green.

By the reign of Henry VIII, the invention of printing had increased, rather than decreased, the number of people learning to write. To some extent, the printing of books removed the need for the scribe, but, as we shall see, the growth of

Plate 5. Maiolica inkstand. North Italian. c.1555–60.

commercial and professional business led to an ever-growing demand for clerks. By the nineteenth century, they formed one of the largest elements of the urban population.

The growing demand for writing skills led to the emergence of a new profession, that of the writing master. He gave advice on choosing quills, cutting and cleaning them, preparing the paper, ruling the lines, and shaping the letters on the page. It was not long before writing masters began to codify their experience in written manuals. Giovanni Battista Palatino published one of the earliest, *Libro nuovo d'imparare a scrivere*, in Rome in 1540, and the first of these books to be printed in London was Jean de Beauchesne's *A Book Containing Divers Sortes of Hands* of 1570. This demonstrated how to write in the roman, italic and secretary hands, and what form of quill to use for each script. Books by writing masters, some of them displaying remarkable virtuosity with the pen, continued to be published until the nineteenth century; probably the best known is George Bickham's *The Universal Penman*, published from 1773 to 1741 *[fig.8]*.

Although the habit of writing spread rapidly in Tudor England, writing equipment remained simple and functional away from the court. From the evidence of portraits, it is clear that there was little attempt to beautify the objects with which most people wrote. The pewter inkwell, for example, with its circular shape and ring of holes seems to have remained unchanged for generations. Paintings from the Italian Renaissance tell the same story. Plain inkpots in the shape of small jars with narrow tops appear in portraits of churchmen and statesmen, while the scribe in Raphael's *Disputa*, taking down St. Augustine's *City of God* from dictation, holds a commonplace portable inkpot.

Among surviving inkstands are a handful of very beautiful sixteenth and seventeenth century examples. The earliest ones take the form of boxes, with hinged lids and a flat top. They are smaller than the writing box, without drawers, and were evidently not intended as a writing support. Many sixteenth century Italian boxes are made of bronze, and decorated with

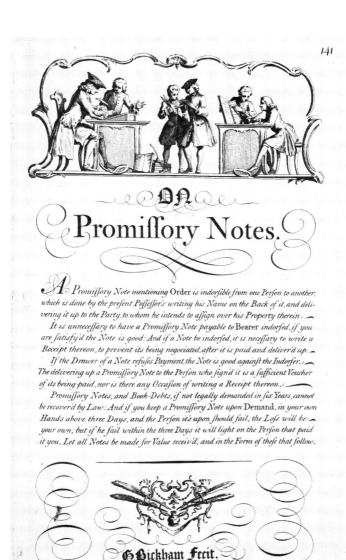

On
Promissory Notes.

A Promissory Note mentioning Order *is indorsible from one Person to another; which is done by the present Possessor's writing his Name on the Back of it, and delivering it up to the Party, to whom he intends to assign over his Property therein.*

It is unnecessary to have a Promissory Note payable to Bearer *indorsed, if you are satisfy'd the Note is good: And if a Note be indorsed, it is necessary to write a Receipt thereon, to prevent its being negociated, after it is paid and deliver'd up.*

If the Drawer of a Note refuses Payment, the Note is good against the Indorser. The delivering up a Promissory Note to the Person who sign'd it is a sufficient Voucher of its being paid, nor is there any Occasion of writing a Receipt thereon.

Promissory Notes, and Book-Debts, if not legally demanded in six Years, cannot be recover'd by Law: And if you keep a Promissory Note upon Demand, in your own Hands above three Days, and the Person it's upon should fail, the Loss will be your own; but if he fail within the three Days it will light on the Person that paid it you. Let all Notes be made for Value receiv'd, and in the Form of these that follow.

G. Bickham Fecit.

N⁰ XXXV.   MDCCXXXVIII.

Figure 8 (opposite). 'Promissory Notes', page from *The Universal Penman* by George Bickham. 1741.

mythological figures. A more delicate example is a large Milanese writing box of the late sixteenth century made of iron, damascened with silver and gilt, in clear imitation of the Islamic style. Inside are three separate containers with their own lids, and a long narrow compartment for pens.

The finest of all Renaissance writing boxes were made in Germany. Various metals were used, and the boxes are often decorated with elaborate patterns or figurative scenes. Sometimes these engravings were purely decorative, but on other occasions an attempt was made to instruct the owner in the Christian virtues. One later sixteenth century brass box tells the writer to beware of evil lust which turns man into an animal, and, to prove the point, a wodwo, a savage beast drawn from folklore, appears on the front, while, on the reverse, a fool is shown breaking up a household. A remarkable ebony example, dated to the late sixteenth century, was decorated and engraved in silver by Theodor de Bry of Frankfurt *[pl.4]*. On the outer lid are roundels representing the four evangelists, while inside are the engraved figures of Moses and Isaiah. The inscription, from St. John's Gospel, refers to the sacred function of writing:

And there are also many things which Jesus did, the which, if they should be written every one, I suppose that even the world itself could not contain the books that should be written. (John XXI, 25)

The hinged box was not, however, the only type of Renaissance inkstand to attract the craftsmen of Italy and Germany. One North Italian example of about 1500 has two containers, but no lid, and it is elaborately decorated with scenes from the life of Coriolanus. More common were compact bronze inkpots, round, square or even triangular, which were made in all parts of Italy in the sixteenth century, and which were accompanied by separate pounce holders. Both often stood on lion feet, and were decorated with grotesques or with animal forms. A popular variety of pounce holder, made in Padua in the later part of the century, is shaped like a frog with a number of shells in which the sand was kept.

More fanciful sixteenth century North Italian inkstands were those made in maiolica, brilliantly painted tin-glazed earthen-ware. Intended for the great and wealthy, many of them displayed considerably virtuosity, and some of the most exceptional were surmounted by sculptured figures. An early, and particularly charming, inkstand has a nativity group mounted on it, while the sand tray rests on the backs of three crouching dogs. This is known to be a very early sixteenth century work by Giovanni Acole of Faenza, but few of the inkstands can be certainly attributed to a particular painter. Another example is decorated with the reclining figure of a sea-god holding a shell for the ink, while a third has a rough copy of the Roman statue of Romulus and Remus with the she-wolf. One of the most interesting, dated 1584, is not sculptured, but has a complex arrangement of wells, each marked with a picture of the implement which belonged there, crossed quills, knives, set-squares, seal-ring, large and small dividers and scissors *[fig.9]*. Later examples were more sophisticated but not without a certain exuberance. One, dating from the early eighteenth century, and made in Angarano, has a figure of St. Gregory the Great rising between two inkholders. If, as seems possible, it once belonged to a great ecclesiastic, he was a man with a secret, for, hidden inside the drawer, an almost invariable element in maiolica inkstands, is a portrait of a smartly-dressed young woman with a lap-dog.

Figure 9. Maiolica inkstand. North Italian 1584.

Figure 10. Silver inkstand. Anthony Nelme. London. About 1685.

Among exceptional examples of these sculptured earthenware inkstands is one made in Northern Italy in about 1480 with incised decoration under a manganese purple glaze. A figure of St. George with the dragon stands on a base with two wells, a small jar for ink, and a candle-holder. Another, made in Bologna in the early sixteenth century, is a much more ostentatious towering work in sgraffito (scratched) ware, its predominant colours of yellow, green, white and brown being less brilliant than those of majolica. Probably made for Costanzo Bentivoglio of Bologna and his wife, Elena Rangoni, it is surmounted by four female figures, two of whom carry shields with their coats of arms.

Most of these earthenware inkwells seem to be trying to disguise their function, and one of the most successful shows an organ player, seated at his instrument, with a spaniel beneath his chair, and with a boy operating the bellows of the organ on the far side *[pl.5]*. Beneath the organ itself was a pen-drawer (now missing), and it is possible that the ink and sand were housed here in separate containers, since no other receptacle was provided for them.

In England, fashion moved more slowly. The earliest surviving English silver inkstands have been dated to the 1630s. Like those on the continent, they were usually in the form of caskets

Figure 11. Brass pen-case. Maden or Madin, Sheffield. 1652.

or boxes, containing various compartments for writing materials. In the late seventeenth century example illustrated here, the outer lid has been abandoned, in favour of four separate containers, attached to a tray. The three square boxes in front are for pounce, wafers and ink, and there is a long one behind for pens *[fig.10]*.

The travelling writing set, developed from the medieval penner, was also popular at this date. In the well-known picture of Charles I with Sir Edmund Walker (National Portrait Gallery), such a set can be seen on the drum that serves as a temporary desk. Compact and round in shape, it comprises a compartment for pens with a top, and a small inkwell, the various units screwing into one another. The picture, which is posthumous, commemorates one of Charles' campaigns in the West Country. Surviving examples of such writing sets vary greatly in quality. The lack of decoration on one example, found near Gloucester Cathedral, and now in the Science Museum, suggests a fairly humble origin. Another, made in Sheffield in 1652, and now in the Victoria and Albert Museum, is elaborately engraved with flower and leaf patterns. The inkwell is here attached to the top of the tube containing the pens, and both are covered by the same hinged lid *[fig.11]*.

4 The Writing Desk

The development of the writing desk is obscure. Writing boxes, like that of Henry VIII, had a sloping lid suitable for writing on, but they were very small. The writing desk, as it developed in England around the end of the sixteenth century, seems to have derived its shape from the medieval lectern. The example illustrated here has a ledge at the base of the sloping surface, suggesting that it was used for reading as well as for writing *[fig.12]*. It is solid, constructed of oak, and patterned with carved vine leaves, grapes and flowers. Inside are spaces for drawers suitable for storing pens, paper and other writing materials. The poet, Sir Thomas Overbury, famous as the victim of an unsolved murder, is shown standing up to write at just such a desk in an engraving of 1613 *[fig.13]*. The young Charles I, when Prince of Wales, had two similar desks covered with red Spanish leather and decorated with gilded patterns, 'a standish above ytt wth Inckpott & dust-box'.

Figure 12. Carved oak desk. English. Early seventeenth century.

THE
Portraicture
of Sir
THOMAS
OVERBVRY
Knight .
ÆTAT. 32.

Renold Elstrack sculpsit

Compton Holland excudit .

Figure 13. Renold Elstracke, *Sir Thomas Overbury*. 1613.

Desks of this kind were useful, but they were far from elegant. New tastes and fashions soon led to the development of an object that was less emphatically solid, and, more important, self-supporting. In the 1670s, the Duke and Duchess of Lauderdale had two walnut writing cabinets made for Ham House, near Richmond. Described as 'scriptors garnished with silver' in the Duchess's inventory, these walnut cabinets, with

Figure 14.
Writing cabinet and stand
veneered with walnut.
English. c.1675.
Ham House.

a patterned veneer, took the form of large boxes, set on an open
stand. When opened, the drop front became a flat writing
surface, with shelves and drawers behind *[fig.14]*. It is said that
the Lauderdales employed Dutch and German cabinet-makers,
and the idea for these desks came from the continent. Another
writing cabinet of similar date has drawers below the drop-leaf
front, as well as a nest inside. The growth of a postal service
meant that more letters were being written, and the design of
the cabinet reflects the need for more space in which to store
them.

The English writing cabinet never reached the ornate and
exuberant forms of continental examples. The magnificent
German Baroque desk shown here was made in 1716 for Gallus
Jacob, an official at the court of the Prince Bishop of Wurzburg
[pl.6]. Veneered with inlaid marquetry in wood, tortoise-shell
and pewter, it is covered all over with drawers and cupboards
which even project at the sides in undulating curves. A superb
work of art, this desk is an appropriate expression of the pomp

and circumstance of a self-important courtier, whose coat of arms it bears on the doors of the central cupboard. Poor Gallus, however, only enjoyed the desk for a brief period. Following the death of the Bishop in 1719, he fell from power, and his goods, which presumably included the desk, were sold to pay the massive fine imposed upon him.

It is not only the owner of this desk whose history is recorded. Due to the chance discovery of a document inside, we know who built it and when. The document reveals that it was the work of two craftsmen, Jacob Arend of Koblentz and Joseph Wittalm of Vienna, who were employed by the court cabinet-maker, Servatius Arend, during the winter of 1715–6. Details of how the desk was made are given. The marquetry, for example, was cut with a fret-saw, and then singed, in the Sander quarter to the south of the city. A touching human note is struck in the complaint that, owing to the war between Austria and Turkey, the two men could not procure meat, and were growing fat on a diet of cabbage and turnips.

The writing cabinet was only one type of desk, current at the time. Another was designed on the gate-leg principle, a writing box top with a leaf supported from below by a gate-leg *[fig.15]*.

Figure 15.
Pine writing desk with gate legs, veneered with walnut and marquetry decoration.
English. 1690.

In 1690, William III and Mary II paid £22.10s to the designer Gerreit Jensen for a 'folding writing table fine markatre with a crowne and cypher'. Jensen was much influenced by French design, and William and Mary themselves were no doubt impressed by life at Versailles, notwithstanding their antipathy to Louis XIV. At the French court, every activity of life was carried out with appropriate style and dignity. Louis' inkwell, made of red jasper and gilt, and surmounted with a fleur de lys, is like an elaborate piece of jewellery (Louvre) *[fig.16]*.

The abundance of surviving eighteenth century furniture reflects the prosperity and comforts of life enjoyed by an ever increasing number of people. This was not only the age of aristocratic elegance, but the age of the expanding middle-classes. Furniture designs were catering both for the great country houses and for those rows of modest Georgian residences which are such a feature of English towns and villages.

Figure 16. Inkstand of Louis XIV. Red jasper and gilt cups in lapis lazuli surmounted by Neptune in silver.

The range and diversity of eighteenth century furniture reflects the variety and complexity of society itself. Different types of desk were designed for different functions, for use in libraries, offices and boudoirs, or, to make a social distinction, for great state rooms as opposed to simple domestic interiors. People were no longer prepared to write on small boxes or ordinary tables. They required specialized pieces of furniture that would decorate and embellish their rooms. The grander and richer they were the more elaborate became their furniture. Looking at the great desks of the eighteenth century, one wonders sometimes if they performed any useful function. Did people really write at them, or were they simply masterpieces of the craftsman's art to be displayed and admired in some grandiose interior?

Unfortunately documentation for eighteenth century desks and writing equipment is scarce. Who made them? when? and for whom? these are questions we can rarely answer, except when documents have been preserved, as in the case of Gallus Jacob's writing cabinet. The presence of a desk in a country house is no guarantee that it has always been there, unless there is supporting evidence in the form of an original bill or receipt. Similarly, the fact that a desk follows a Chippendale design is no evidence of its maker, since Chippendale designs circulated freely in contemporary workshops. Silver inkstands are sometimes stamped with the date and name of the maker, and even occasionally with the coat of arms of the first owner, but for those in baser materials there are few or no identifying marks. The objects survive, but without a personal history to illumine them.

When discussing eighteenth century desks, it is often difficult to define contemporary terminology. The sécretaire in France meant a bureau with a writing flap that could be pulled out, but, in England, it was applied to writing-tables of every kind. Similarly, the term escritoire, used to describe French writing cabinets of the late seventeenth century, passed into English common parlance as meaning any form of desk with a lock.

The most popular type of desk in England in the early

eighteenth century was probably the bureau. (The word bureau was originally derived from bure, the name of the type of coarse cloth used in the Middle Ages to cover the tables and chests at which the clerks wrote.) This was a relatively large piece constructed in three parts: a chest of drawers below, a writing desk in the middle and a cabinet above. The desk was usually a derivation of the old-fashioned writing box, with a sloping top that opened outwards to form the writing surface, supported from below. In some bureaux there was no sloping top. Instead a large drawer pulled forward with a hinged front that came down to make a writing flap. Variations later in the century included the substitution of cupboards for drawers below, and bookshelves for cupboards above or the omission of the upper stage altogether. From France came the concept of the roll top; the curved top slid up and over into a recess behind. This type is still known by its French name, bureau à cylindre.

The bureau was made in a variety of materials and styles, although it was always distinguished by a certain simplicity and elegance of line. Among the most striking examples are those covered with Japanese lacquer, or with a walnut veneer. Mirror panels and glass-fronted doors helped to relieve the effect of height and solidity. The upper stage is sometimes decorated with Corinthian pilasters, and even with a pediment, in imitation of classical architecture. An example of this kind is the desk said to have belonged to Jonathan Swift, where two pairs of marquetry pilasters frame the looking glasses *[fig.17]*. Beneath each of the pilasters is a highly formalised marquetry pattern, with scrollwork surrounding a griffin. The rather severe appearance of the bureau may be due to the loss of its original superstructure, with pediment and figures.

The bureau was a piece of furniture designed to stand against the wall. More suitable for large public rooms was the so-called library table, a free-standing desk with two nests of drawers below, separated by an arched opening, that could be used on either side. Such tables were elaborate in form and decoration, and they were produced for large aristocratic houses.

The writing table presents yet another contrast in form and

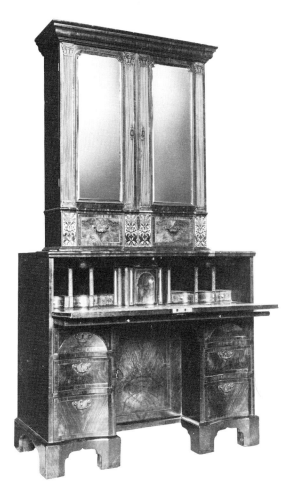

Figure 17. Writing cabinet with a walnut veneer. Possibly Irish.
Early eighteenth century. Said to have belonged to Jonathan Swift.

function. The true writing table had no drawers or cupboards
above the writing surface. Those below were arranged in a
variety of ways, often with a recessed space in the middle to
accommodate knees. However, it was common to recess the

drawers of ordinary cabinets in this way, and it is easy to mistake them for the true desk. The typical French eighteenth century writing table called a bureau plat had an elegant writing surface, often patterned with marquetry, standing on four gently curving legs. Ormolu or bronze mounts frequently framed the writing surface, and accentuated the elegant form of the legs. Locks, and other decorative features were frequently picked out and marked with gilded scrolls. An engraving by Baquoy, after a painting by Moreau le Jeune of 1776, presents a delightful picture of the French writing table in use. The anxious father is awaiting the birth of his child and occupying the time with his books while seated at his writing table *[fig.18]*. We see him as the nurse appears with the happy news. 'C'est un fils, monsieur', carrying with her a baby which cannot be less than three months old. The table is long and curving, with the characteristic bronze lip along the edge, an elegant device to prevent papers from blowing or sliding off. Because the writing table had little space for storing papers and letters, a separate piece of furniture, a cartonnier, was frequently used in conjunction with it. The cartonnier, which contained a number of drawers and pigeon holes, either stood next to the writing table, like a tall cabinet, or was placed on one end of the table itself.

It is significant that in French and English literary portraits, sitters are invariably shown at writing tables as opposed to bureaux. Desks of the latter kind are mostly seen in the portraits of well-to-do tradesmen, especially those in the low countries. Clearly, a rich tradesman, with voluminous documents and bills would need a capacious desk. However, it is always dangerous to accept pictures uncritically as evidence of the way in which people lived, since artists often rely on pictorial conventions rather than their own experience.

In England, as elsewhere, writing tables varied greatly in elegance. A receipt for a mahogany writing table supplied by Chippendale to Paxton House in 1774, describes it as having two flaps, 'the middle part covered with Cloath and made to rise & drawers for papers, pen, Ink, sand etc. on Castors . . . £3.8.0d' *[fig.19]*. We tend to judge eighteenth century desks by

Figure 18. C. Baquoy after Moreau le Jeune, *C'est un fils, Monsieur.*
1776.

the splendid examples which survive in museums and country
houses, but the majority of desks, like this one, must have been
simple and functional in form, and, of course, inexpensive.

Among the most refined of all eighteenth century writing
tables are those designed for women. Again, it was the French
who led the rest of Europe. Small desks on thin legs, with a few
drawers and pigeon holes, became an essential piece of furniture
for the fasionable lady's boudoir. Often given the delightful

Figure 19. Mahogany writing table. Thomas Chippendale. 1774.

name, 'bonheur du jour', these pretty pieces of furniture, veneered or decorated with panels of porcelain, frequently seem too slight for their function.

Simpler, but still essentially feminine, are the French writing tables of the later eighteenth century, which consist of a low oval table with one small drawer. The German designer, David Roentgen, who worked at Koblentz on the Rhine, specialised in these tables which he exported all over Europe, even as far as Russia. One of his desks, made in the 1780s, has a scene from Virgil's *Aeneid* on the top, while others are patterned with flowers and leaves.

The luxury and frivolity of the French aristocracy is nowhere better demonstrated than in their secrétaire toilettes, a combination of desk and dressing table. The example shown here is covered with marquetry designs of buildings and musical instruments *[pl.7]*. When the writing shelf is pulled forward, the front rises, revealing drawers behind. The space for writing materials is clearly subsidiary to those for cosmetics and perfumes, which were housed in the large lower drawer, and the presence of a mirror inside the lid of one drawer completes the impression of worldliness.

Evidence about ladies' desks in contemporary literature is less than one might expect, considering the importance of letter-writing in the plots of so many contemporary novels. The characters in Samuel Richardson's novels, *Pamela* and *Clarissa*, are forever engaged in writing letters to one another, but there is little precise descriptive detail. We learn in one passage that Clarissa, an heiress, has an escritoire with a lockable drawer, where she keeps the letters of her lover, Lovelace. The low English mahogany writing table of about 1750 illustrated here *[fig.20]*, with its marquetry panels, and small drawers is similar in type to such an escritoire. On top of Clarissa's desk is a standish, with ink, pounce and pens. In order to stop her writing letters, Clarissa's parents remove the standish, as well as a parcel of pens, and half a pint of ink. The prudent girl, however, has carefully hidden a supply of crow-quill pens, and the corre-spondence continues.

Figure 20. Mahogany desk. English. c.1750.

The profound change in taste from the frivolous rococo to the severe neo-classic, accentuated by the French Revolution of 1789, brought about inevitable changes in the style and form of French furniture. The secrétaire à abattant, an upright wall desk with a rectangular drop front, had already been introduced at the court of Louis XVI, and it remained popular throughout the Empire period. It was decorated in ormolu with classical devices typical of the time, caryatids, swans and pilasters. Another example is the upright secrétaire made in Paris in about 1790, and attributed to the master cabinet-maker, Bernard Molitor *[pl.8]*. The secrétaire has a simple drop front above, which conceals the drawers inside, and has two plain cupboards below. It is remarkable for its bronze decorations, which gain in effect from the comparative simplicity of the style, and from the exceptionally high quality of the wood, oak veneered with mahogany. Molitor himself is known to have been one of the designers who survived the revolutionary period between Louis XVI and Napoleon, and he flourished under the new régime.

The great authors of the eighteenth century rarely mention their desks, nor do they often appear in the literary portraits of the time. In his journal of 1712, Swift records that Lady Orkney has ordered him a writing table as a present. He is shown composing at a desk like this in the well-known portrait of him by Charles Jervas, and not at a bureau like the one shown at figure 17 which he is said to have owned.

The extremely simple desk at which Dr. Johnson wrote his great dictionary is at Pembroke College, Oxford, rescued from destruction by a public appeal in the Victorian period. Johnson certainly believed in the importance of a good desk. 'Composing a dictionary requires books and a desk', he once wrote, 'you can make a poem walking in the fields or lying in bed.'

In his biography of another poet, Johnson records that Pope 'punctually required that his writing-box should be set upon his bed before he rose ... Lord Oxford's domestick related that, in the dreadful winter of Forty, she was called from her bed by him four times in one night, to supply him with paper, lest he should lose a thought'. The old-fashioned writing box had not

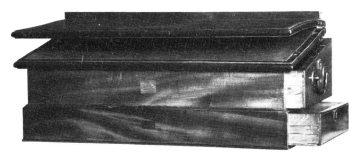

Figure 21. Mahogany writing box. Eighteenth century. Once the property of Oliver Goldsmith.

been completely ousted by the desk, and was still employed, both for travelling and, as in Pope's case, for ease of conveyance around the house. These boxes remained popular for many years, and, like the larger bureaux, they were often made of walnut or japanned. The mahogany box illustrated here, with a folding top and two drawers, once belonged to Oliver Goldsmith *[fig.21]*.

Voltaire, living in exile on the Lake of Geneva, is reported to have had five desks in his bedroom at Ferney. Notes relating to the various subjects at which he was working were carefully arranged on each, plays, essays, novels and so forth. Voltaire also took an interest in his writing chair. At the end of his life, he ordered one with a moveable writing leaf attached to one arm, and a nest of drawers on the other. His companion, Madame de Chatelet, boasted an amber desk which had been given to her by Frederick the Great.

5 The Inkstand

The inkstands that stood on eighteenth century desks were designed to set them off, and they were, in consequence, often elaborately decorated. For sheer exuberance and panache there are none to match those made in France. Early eighteenth century inkstands are relatively restrained, like the example in gold and brilliant blue, made in the style of Boulle, which is inlaid with brass and tortoiseshell *[pl.9]*. The later rococo designers of the Louis Quinze period found it easy to run riot on such a small scale. A design for an 'écritoire de porcelaine' by Juste-Aurèle Meissonnier, shows the extremes that might be aimed at, with its curling shell shapes for the two well disguised containers *[fig.22]*. Rococo designs were publicised through engravings, and Meissonnier's fanciful style was echoed all over Europe. The porcelain example illustrated here was made at Frankenthal in Germany in the mid eighteenth century in the chinoiserie style. Even the necessary containers are rendered delightful by concealing two of them under fantastic lids, in the shape of a pair of Chinamen *[pl.10]*.

In England, inkstands, like writing desks, were far less ornate. At the end of the seventeenth century, the exiled Huguenot goldsmiths had introduced a new style of inkstand, which achieved rapid popularity. As opposed to the inkstand in a box, this was a tray with inkpot and pounce pot, not unlike the containers on a cruet. In front was a space for pens, penknives and wafers. A bell to call a servant or a candleholder sometimes stood in the centre *[fig.23]*. While standishes, as these inkstands were called, reflected changes in style, from rococo to neoclassical and regency, the basic layout remained unchanged until the end of the nineteenth century. Glass, porcelain and pottery standishes, popular from the late eighteenth century, were generally based on silver prototypes.

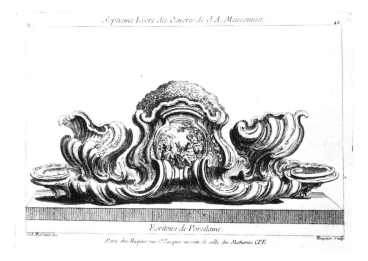

Ecritoire de Porcelaine.

Paris chez Huquier rue S.^tJacque au coin de celle des Mathurins CPR.

Figure 22. Juste-Aurèle Meissonnier. Design for an inkstand of porcelain.

Figure 23. Silver inkstand by Paul de Lamerie. 1729–30.

45

Of exceptional quality are the porcelain standishes made by the Chelsea and Derby factories in the middle of the eighteenth century. Typical are those with two containers surmounted by elegant lids, which stand at either end of a narrow tray. Between them is a thin taper holder, and behind a shortish box, presumably for wafers, not pens. The dark blue ground of the example illustrated here, is set off by delightfully painted butterflies and birds. The handle of the wafer box, is modelled as a lamb, a wreath of red and yellow flowers hung round its neck *[pl.11]*. Such a delicacy was typical of the 1760s. Later on the scale becomes broader. In inkstands of the Bloor Derby period dated to the 1820s the containers stand between two deep ridges where the pen rested. They are decorated with landscape scenes in the manner of the water-colourists of the period. In one example rural scenes are depicted, a cottage under trees and a man crossing a bridge by a waterfall, and another has a view of the Royal Hospital at Greenwich, and a river scene with a bridge.

Not everybody could afford an elegant standish, and cheaper inkwells, made by the Bow and Lowestoft factories, were of a much simpler design. One, which bears the inscription, 'made at New Canton (the Bow factory) in 1751', is more like the earlier pewter inkwells of the Jacobean period *[fig.24]*. It is

Figure 24.
Inkstand.
Bow. 1751.

46

round, with the familiar five holes for quill pens, surrounding the inkwell itself. This particular inkstand may have been used as an advertising sample, to be given away to customers and friends of the new factory. Decorated with sprays of flowers in the oriental style, it revealed something of the quality of the wares, but in a simple and uncomplicated form. Early ceramic inkwells manufactured by Wedgwood in the 1770s repeat this simple formula. One earthenware inkwell, with a charming rustic pattern, has the name of its owner 'Mary Adams', and the date '1772' painted on.

Square and heart-shaped inkwells were a popular form in earthenware, particularly in France. The novelist Alain-Fournier, writing in the early part of the twentieth century, describes an 'old fashioned inkwell in the shape of a heart', in his delightful novel, *Le Grand Meaulnes*. Rather more sophisticated examples of traditional faience are inkstands in the form of trays, with two raised containers behind, and a drawer for wafers between them. The example illustrated is decorated with a simply drawn Harlequin and an oriental looking tree. Flower patterns, and two crossed quill pens also appear, with further oriental motifs on the sides *[pl.12]*.

A few of the writers of the period are shown with pen and ink, but it is unwise to conclude that the equipment shown in the portrait was their own. Michael Dahl portrays Joseph Addison with a peculiarly pleasing square silver inkstand, but, since it appears again in a portrait of another sitter, it was presumably simply a studio prop. Most of the writers regarded pen and ink as a means to an end, rather than as objects in their own right. Noting a slackening of pace in the composition of his novel, *Tristram Shandy*, Laurence Sterne tells us that 'this moment that I last dipp'd my pen into my ink, I could not help taking notice what a cautious air of sad composure and solemnity there appear'd in my manner of doing it'. How different, he says, from his practice when truly engaged with his work: 'dropping thy pen – spurting thy ink about thy table and thy books – as if thy pen and thy ink, thy books and furniture cost thee nothing!'

Goethe on the other hand, was a martinet when it came to composition. In his house in Weimar, he kept a special room for writing, with plain pinewood shelves and cabinets, and hard chairs. He always dictated to one of three copyists, pacing up and down as he did so, but he was none the less demanding about the exact conditions of their work. The quill pens had to be cut neither too long nor too short, and the plume of feathers had to be completely removed. While the young Goethe, scribbling down impressions on his Italian journey, thought nothing of dipping his pen into the sepia paint of an artist friend, the older Goethe insisted that the inkpot must never be too full, that there should be no inkstains, that the page should be dried in front of the stove and not with sand, and that small squares of paper should be used to seal his letters, to prevent the wax from damaging them. These operations had to be carried out smoothly and quietly so as not to disturb the great man's concentration. Goethe himself had been taught to write by a writing master, Magister artis scribendi, who came to his father's house. Clear and careful handwriting was a lifelong obsession with Goethe, while his spelling and punctuation remained erratic and inconsistent.

A revealing source for practical information about writing materials and their cost is the diary of the obscure Norfolk clergyman, James Woodforde, written during the last quarter of the eighteenth century. In 1759, while still an Oxford undergraduate, he records buying 'of Mr. Prince the Bookseller in New College Lane, a standish with Sand, Ink, Wafers and half a hundred of Pens'. Sadly he does not give the price of the standish, but forty years later, he tells us that he paid 1s 6d for a '¼ Hundred of new pens', and that he had some old ones 'mended' for 6d. Woodforde regularly records the costs of wafers (3d or 4d a box), steel sand (5d a paper), and of two inkstands, one for carrying in the pocket (1s 6d) and then a black Wedgwood example, bought in 1802, which proved to be too small (1s 0d). In 1783, he mentions the purchase of what he describes as a 'pretty pocket leather inkhorn' for his niece.

Woodforde's equipment was relatively modest. Charles

Lamb's nostalgic memories of the clerks of the South Sea House, where he worked briefly in 1792, suggest that professional scribes wanted to cut more of a dash. Lamb was struck, in retrospect, by the very size of their possessions: 'The heavy, odd-shaped ivory-handled penknives (our ancestors had everything on a larger scale than we have hearts for) are as good as anything from Herculaneum. The pounce-boxes of our days have gone retrograde.' Of one of his fellow-clerks, Woolett, Lamb recalls: 'How profoundly would he nib a pen–with what deliberation would he wet a wafer.'

From the South Sea House, Lamb went to work in the East India House, where Thomas De Quincey once saw him sitting upon an absurdly high stool, for whose altitude De Quincey could 'imagine no possible use or sense'. Perhaps no one gives us such a keen sense of the life of a clerk as Charles Dickens. He had himself worked as a junior clerk for just over a year, and the high broad desk at which he sat is preserved at Dickens House in London. In his picture of Newman Noggs in *Nicholas Nickleby*, and of Bob Cratchit in *A Christmas Carol*, Dickens provides his immortal archetypes of the clerk. Towards the end of his career, Dickens created Jarvis Lorry, the cheerful chief clerk of Tellson's bank in *A Tale of Two Cities*. In his illustration to this novel, Phiz captures the scene at the bank, with admirable succinctness, the steep desks, high stools, ledgers, boxes, quills and inkpots. The novel is set back in the late eighteenth century, but Phiz had no need to go outside the limits of his own century for illustrative material *[fig.25]*.

The writing style of the clerks was that which we know as copperplate, a hand originally developed, as its name implies, for etching on copper. From the later eighteenth century to the early twentieth, all documents were laboriously copied in this style. At the very end of this period, the poet, Robert Bridges, referred to the writing of clerks in lawyers' offices as having 'scrupulously perfected the very most ugly thing that a conscientious civilisation has ever perpetrated'.

In the earlier part of the nineteenth century, the seemingly immortal quill still held sway throughout Europe. In his *Diary*

Plate 7. Lady's desk and Dressing Table, veneered with marquetry of various woods. Paris. c.1777.

Plate 6 (opposite).
Pine writing cabinet veneered with marquetry of various woods, tortoiseshell and pewter. Servatius Arend. Craftsmen Joseph Wittalm of Vienna and Jacob Arend of Koblentz. Wurzburg. 1716.

Plate 8. Upright secrétaire in oak veneered with mahogany.
Attributed to Bernard Molitor. Paris. c.1790.

Plate 9. Inkstand with marquetry in the style of Boulle. French.
Early eighteenth century.

Plate 10. Inkstand. Model attributed to J. W. Lanz. Frankenthal.
c.1756.

53

Plate 13. Papier-maché writing box and blotter. English. Box, mid nineteenth century, blotter, 1851.

Plate 11 (top opposite). Inkstand. Chelsea. c.1765. Schreiber Collection.

Plate 12 (bottom opposite). Inkstand in tin glazed earthenware. French. c.1770.

Figure 25. Phiz (Hablot Knight Browne), 'Mr Stiver at Tellson's Bank', an illustration to *A Tale of Two Cities* by Charles Dickens. 1859.

of a Madman, the Russian writer, Gogol, tells us of an unfortunate clerk who has to sharpen twenty-three quills for the director of his office 'who likes to have a lot of pens', and four more for the director's daughter. On a lighter note, Jane Austen describes Caroline Bingley in *Pride and Prejudice*, desperately trying to attract the attention of the hero, who is writing a letter: 'I am afraid you do not like your pen. Let me mend it for you. I mend pens remarkably well.' She is firmly snubbed with the reply: 'Thank you–but I always mend my own.' In *Mansfield Park*, Fanny Price requires the assistance of her cousin, Edmund Bertram, who 'prepared her paper', 'ruled her lines', and 'continued with her the whole time of her writing, to assist her with his penknife or his orthography'.

6 The Pen-Nib

Sharpening quill pens with a penknife, shaking the pounce pot or sand box (now full of chalk or magnesia as a blotting agent), sticking on a wafer to fasten the letter, these activities, mentioned by Richardson, Woodforde, Lamb, Jane Austen and Dickens, must have seemed immemorial and eternal.

As in so many things, so in writing equipment the nineteenth century witnessed a series of minor revolutions. The invention of blotting-paper rendered the preparation of the paper and the pounce pot redundant. So strong is convention, however, that a second inkpot was frequently substituted for the pounce box, thus preserving the symmetrical shape of the inkstand. With the spread of letter writing, the gummed envelope was developed, and it slowly superseded the wafer.

These were merely the accessories. With the invention of the steel pen-nib the nineteenth century triumphed. Metal pens had been appearing since Roman times, but they were rigid, and difficult to use. If you owned a metal pen, it was a prized possession rather than a practical tool. Thus, in 1790, Parson Woodforde notes, 'this wrote with a Copper Pen, late my mother's', and, in 1810, Lord Byron tells his correspondent that he is writing with a gold pen which he has received as a gift.

At first, a steel pen was no more flexible than a copper or gold one, but refinements were gradually introduced. A number of inventors had a part to play in this process, but the man who probably did most to popularise the steel nib was Joseph Gillott, the Birmingham pen-manufacturer, who started life as a button-maker. Gillott is said to have discovered that he could use techniques learnt in making buttons to produce steel pen-nibs, and he patented an example in 1831. Ironically, Gillott himself was probably illiterate, but 'His Nibs' completely transformed the activity of writing for several generations. The steel nib, fitted into a pen-holder, was far more durable than the quill, although corrosion from the ink did result in slow deterioration.

We could find no better account of the trials and tribulations of using a steel nib than that contained in the diary of Virginia Woolf. She was profoundly affected by the physical circumstances of her art. As a young woman, wishing to emulate her sister, the painter Vanessa Bell, she devised a desk at which she could stand to write, and, in 1933, she records her delight in 'having after only ten years or so, made myself, in five minutes, a perfect writing board, with pen tray attached, so that I can't ever again fly into a fury bereft of ink and pen at the most critical moment of a writer's life and see my sudden sentence dissipate itself all for lack of a pen handy'.

For Virginia Woolf, a new nib or pen was a positive incentive to creation: 'I will take a new pen and new page' she says on one occasion, or 'Yes, I will allow myself a new nib' on another. For a generation used to the ball-point pen, her tribulations seem remote: 'Whenever I suck my pen' she says, 'my lip is covered with ink. And I have no ink with which to fill my pot'. If a new pen or nib meant a surge of inspiration to her, an old one could cause her to lose momentum. 'I am writing with a pen which is feeble and wispy', she records in October 1927, as she rejects the idea of drawing up a plan of work, and, in May 1938, struggling with the uncongenial task of writing a biography of her friend, Roger Fry, she reports: 'the worst spring on record; my pens diseased, even the new box . . . what am I going to say with a defective nib?' That sense of the moment, which is so characteristic of her work as a novelist, makes her record the completion of a major novel in these terms: 'I have just finished, with this very nib-ful of ink, the last sentence of *The Waves*.'

Virginia Woolf is, naturally enough, concerned with the efficacy of her pen-nib. Other less dedicated writers were intrigued by the pen-holder. The possibilities of designing new pen-holders were almost limitless, and children, in particular, were constantly competing for novelties. In *Le Grand Meaulnes*, Alain-Fournier records the arrival of a vagabond boy, who impressed the others with his:

'picture' pen-holders ... if you closed one eye you could see, through an eyelet in the handle, an enlarged if somewhat blurred view of the Basilica of Lourdes or some less familiar monument.

While the master's back is turned, the boys gaze into the pen-holder to see 'a glaucous and spotty view of Notre Dame de Paris'.

Le Grand Meaulnes is one of the more attractive accounts of education in this period. At Salem House, David Copperfield's first school, the exercise of writing has left 'a dirty atmosphere of ink surrounding all ... There could not well be more ink splashed about it, if it had been roofless from its first construction, and the skies had rained, snowed, hailed and blown ink through the varying seasons of the year'.

A charming evocation of the sheer drudgery of learning to write is to be found in a painting of a young girl by Henriette Browne, a French artist of the mid nineteenth century *[fig.26]*.

Figure 26. Henriette Browne, *Interior: a girl writing at a table.* Mid nineteenth century.

The girl has been set the uncongenial task of copying out a passage from a book. Her boredom is evident. She has been gathering flowers in the fresh air, and now, trapped inside, she is more concerned with her pet bird than with her pen, which hangs limply from her hand. A sheet of grubby blotting paper underlines the fact that she is no expert.

If the spread of the steel nib simplified writing in the nineteenth century, it did not lead to clearer desks, which were often crowded with a host of small and useful objects. There was the paper knife and the glass paperweight, often produced as souvenirs and decorated with pictures of seaside resorts and beauty spots. The pen wiper and the blotting book were usually hand made, and given away as Christmas and birthday presents *[pl.13]*. Additional accessories included the rack for writing paper and envelopes, and the pen rest.

Figure 27. A typical advertisement for steel pens which appeared in the advertisement section of the *Illustrated Catalogue of the Industrial Department, British Section,* International Exhibition of 1862.

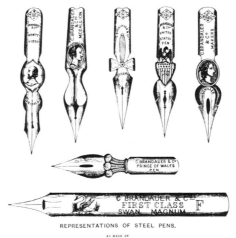

REPRESENTATIONS OF STEEL PENS.

AS MADE BY

C. BRANDAUER & CO.

Manufacturers of Steel Pens of every description,

NEW JOHN STREET PEN WORKS,

BIRMINGHAM.

7 Victorian and Modern

This account of Victorian clutter might lead one to suppose that the writing desks of the period were fussy and over decorated. The history of Victorian furniture design is, however, extremely complex, and it is hard to generalise at all about a period so rich in variations of style. Early Victorian design is characterised by a strong historicist sense, at its most successful and most prevalent in the Gothic revival, but also revealing itself in furniture inspired by Elizabethan, neo-classical or even rococo originals. Later in the period came the Aesthetic Movement, a return to a consciously simple and artistic style. The spread of mass production meant that changes in design were far more swiftly assimilated by the general public than ever before, and modified or debased examples of the works of the great designers rapidly made their appearance in the homes of the middle classes.

The most interesting desks of the period were not the commercial products to be found in the shops, but those individually designed by leading architects and designers. In the 1840s, A. W. N. Pugin produced Gothic style desks for the Palace of Westminster, and, at the end of the century, George Jack was designing a desk in the 'arts and crafts' style for Morris and Co. The fine desk made by Thomas Jeckyll in the 1870s as part of a suite of furniture for A.A. (Alecco) Ionides, the Greek merchant and collector, was a special commission [fig.28]. With its ebony mouldings and brass mounts it combines oriental details with classic Victorian design. It has a wide range of drawers and cupboards, their contrasting shapes and sizes accentuated by the balance of light and dark wood. It is not just a piece of abstract design, but a well conceived and coherent piece of furniture, ideally adapted for its function.

Totally different in style, but again of the highest quality is

Figure 28. Walnut desk. Thomas Jeckyll. c.1875.

a desk designed by C. F. A. Voysey some twenty years later
[fig.29]. Where the accent in the Jeckyll desk is on width, and
on variations of surface and texture, Voysey's design is essentially vertical and almost exaggeratedly plain. Made in oak, it
rises on four thin legs, with a simple writing surface, and a
single cupboard over it. The only decoration is to be found on
the cupboard door, where the copper hinges are the dominant
feature. This desk emphatically rejects the idea of small pigeon
holes and drawers, and returns to the idea of the simple function
of writing, a design idea which has been carried into the
twentieth century.

Although the nineteenth century is generally associated with
the development of devices which were intended to make
writing easier, it was also, paradoxically, an age in which fine
calligraphy was revived for its own sake. Although earlier
scholars, like Horace Walpole, had collected manuscripts, and
although the tradition of illuminating formal documents had
never entirely died out, it was not until the nineteenth century
that designers like Owen Jones and Pugin began to try to imitate

medieval scripts and, in some cases, to publish the results of their work.

As in so many things, William Morris was a pioneer. He began to create his own illuminated manuscripts in 1856, writing in a pointed Gothic style, but for some years this interest was submerged by others. Morris came back to it in the early 1870s, when he did his best calligraphic work. He cut his own quill pens, and developed a rounded version of the italic writing of the Italian fifteenth century. Morris had a considerable effect on the revival of calligraphy, but it was an indirect one. The most important direct impetus was given by Edward Johnston, whose *Writing and Illuminating and Lettering* appeared in 1906. Through Johnston's example, calligraphy began to be taught in art schools, and today many children learn the italic script which is widely practised, both by amateur enthusiasts and by professionals.

Figure 29.
Oak writing desk.
C. F. A. Voysey. 1896.

This movement was not confined to Britain. In his novel, *The Idiot*, of 1869, Dostoyevsky describes how his hero, Prince Myshkin, who is being considered for an office job, tells a hot-tempered general that he is something of a calligrapher, and then settles down to prove his skill by writing passages in a variety of scripts from a number of different countries and centuries. His masterpiece is a sentence in the medieval Russian hand.

A very different writer, the young Evelyn Waugh, also took an interest in calligraphy and actually won a prize for an illuminated manuscript at Lancing College in 1919. Waugh's enthusiasm came from a meeting with Edward Johnston two years before:

I was fourteen and Johnston was forty-five when I was taken to see him. He received me with exquisite charm and demonstrated how to cut a turkey-quill into a chisel-pointed pen ... The art of the scribe is sometimes considered spinsterish. The sweep and precision of Johnston's strokes were as virile as a bull-fighter's and left me breathless.

Waugh's victory in the writing competition led to his being allowed to visit Francis Crease, an amateur calligrapher, on one half holiday a week. Under Crease's supervision, Waugh half-heartedly pursued his interest, bored by the effort, but delighted at the chance of getting out of school.

The nineteenth century was the great age of the novelist, who could be expected to spend many hours labouring over his desk. A famous travelling one was designed by Anthony Trollope, so that he could continue writing during his frequent train journeys as a post office official. It was a sloping box, not dissimilar to the portable desks of the early seventeenth century. The desk came to a sad end on Trollope's trip to North America in the 1860s, an event which he described in a moving eulogy:

I shall never forget my agony as I saw and heard my desk fall from a porter's hand on a railway station, as he tossed it from him seven yards off on to the hard pavement. I heard its poor weak intestines rattle in their death-struggle, and knowing it was smashed I forgot my position on American soil and remonstrated.

Trollope was laughed at for his pains: 'So I gathered up the broken article, and deplored the ill-luck which had brought me to so savage a country.'

Another famous novelist, Charles Dickens, was painted by W. P. Frith seated at his desk in a self-consciously literary pose [fig.30]. The setting is Dickens' study at Tavistock Terrace, the date 1859. The small desk with a sloping writing surface and a flap at the side to hold books and papers is said still to exist in

Figure 30. William Powell Frith, *Charles Dickens in his study at Tavistock House.* 1859.

Figure 31. After Sir Luke Fildes. *The Empty Chair, Gad's Hill –
Ninth of June 1870*. From *The Graphic*, 25 December 1870.

Philadelphia. Open on top of it is the manuscript of *A Tale of
Two Cities*, and beyond a rack for paper and pens, a calendar
and a framed address of congratulation from the citizens of
Birmingham. The creative artist in his study is a favourite
theme with Victorian portraitists. Frith's characterization of
Dickens is a rather complacent and flattering one, compared
with the haunted expression of contemporary photographs, but
it shows him in familiar surroundings with the tools of his trade.

In his last years, when he lived at Gad's Hill Place, Dickens
usually worked at an enormous desk crowded with pigeon holes
and drawers, and with a central writing slope. In the illustration
by Luke Fildes for *The Graphic*, published soon after the
novelist's sudden death in 1870, and entitled *The Empty Chair*,
we see a row of knick-knacks along the top of the desk, including
a glass inkwell, a magnifying glass, and the china monkey which
was the novelist's mascot [*fig.31*]. All of these and the desk itself
survive at Dickens House, as does the chair which is identical
with that in the Frith portrait. The novelist did not write his
last words at this desk, but on the smaller writing table in the
garden chalet. A photograph of the interior of this charming
folly shows a plain table with a portable writing slope placed on

it, the former being now at Dickens House, the latter in the Victoria and Albert Museum.

The survival of so many desks and chairs belonging to Dickens is an indication not only of his extraordinary popularity, but of the importance which his admirers attached to such relics. In the museums which were established to commemorate great writers, desks and pens are among the most prominent items on display. The County Museum in Dorchester, for example, has reconstructed Thomas Hardy's study, and the centre-piece is the large desk at which he wrote. The row of pens and inkpots have now a certain period charm, for already in Hardy's lifetime, novelists had the typewriter at their disposal, although, to begin with, few of them actually composed directly onto it.

Attempts had been made to develop a typewriter since the eighteenth century, originally as a means of helping the blind, but the first commercially viable machine was manufactured by Remingtons in America in the 1870s. The public were slow to realise the potential of the new machine, and it was not until the 1880s, that the market for typewriters began to develop. The

Figure 32.
A Williams typewriter of 1892.
It was the smallest practical
machine produced up to that date.

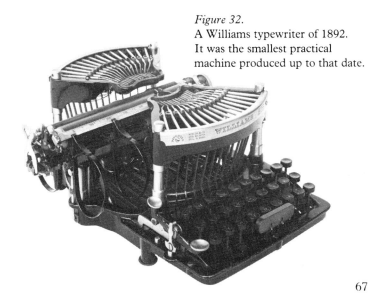

early typewriters had some inevitable problems connected with the movement of the paper and the inking, but, once the demand began to grow, modifications and improvements were rapidly introduced. The most significant recent development has been the advent of the electric typewriter, in the 1930s.

We naturally connect the typewriter with the modern office, where the female typist has replaced the male clerk. It was once thought very dashing to be a secretary, and Arnold Bennett's heroine, Hilda Lessways, helps to establish her claim as a modern woman by being the first woman to be so employed in the Five Towns.

One of the most celebrated literary figures to be associated with the typewriter is Henry James, who is sometimes said to have changed his style because of it. James never actually learnt to type, however. In his early years he submitted his work to the publisher in longhand, and later he sent his manuscripts to an agency for typing. Then, in 1896, he began to suffer from what was probably writer's cramp, and so he began to dictate directly to a typist. From then onwards 'Remingtonese', as James himself called it, became a pronounced element in his famous 'later manner' as a novelist. His biographer, Leon Edel, notes that

Henry James writing, and Henry James dictating, were two different artists. His sentences were to become, in time, elaborate—one might indeed say baroque—filled with qualifications and parentheses.

The typewriter, far from being a liberating influence for James, actually restricted him, since a large Remington, and a typist, were not easy things to carry about. In June 1897, he wanted to get off to Italy:

The voice of Venice, all this time, has called very loud. But it has been drowned a good deal in the click of the typewriter to which I dictate and which, some months ago, crept into my existence through the crevice of a lame hand and now occupies in it a place too big to be left vacant for long periods of hotel and railway life.

If the nineteenth century produced the steel nib and the typewriter, the twentieth century brought the latter to a very high level technically, and, in addition, found its own aid to easier writing, the ball-point pen. The disadvantages of dipping a pen into ink are obvious, and, during the nineteenth century, efforts were made to develop a reservoir or fountain pen, where the ink is contained in a barrel inside the stem, from which it flows onto the nib in a steady stream. A workable model had appeared by the 1900s, and the fountain pen, with many refinements, is still with us today. At much the same time, inventors were also experimenting with the idea of the ball-point pen, and the first satisfactory model was developed in the 1930s by a Hungarian living in Argentina, Laszlo Biro. The ball-point pen has a revolving ball at the tip, which rolls through ink contained inside the pen, and deposits it evenly onto the paper. This discovery has been the greatest revolution in writing since the quill pen itself, and it has rendered the last remaining implements, ink and blotting paper, as obsolete as the penknife and the pounce pot.

Figure 33. Desk and chair designed by Sir Ambrose Heal. 1929.

One might indeed question whether writing itself is not in danger of becoming obsolete. All business letters and papers, and many private ones, are now being typed rather than written, and the private letter has, in any case, been dealt a severe blow by the telephone. Calligraphy, or fine handwriting, is now regarded as an art, rather than as a part of normal life, and the writing desk or bureau is by no means an essential piece of furniture in the small houses or flats of our day.

Before we begin a lamentation for writing, however, we should recall that it has always been a means to an end, an aid to human communication, rather than a self-regarding art. The basic instincts which writing satisfies are not passing out of existence, they are merely finding other means of expression, which will doubtless lead man into paths as varied and extraordinary as those in his past history. We may regret that so much of the style and beauty have gone, and that the desks and inkwells illustrated here have become collectors' pieces, divorced from their original function, but great works of literature are still appearing, even with the aid of such soulless artefacts as the ball-point pen and the typewriter, and there is no reason to suppose that they will cease to do so.